Silkies

and Other Guinea Pigs

Editor in Chief: Paul A. Kobasa
Supplementary Publications: Shawn Brennan, Lisa Kwon, Christine Sullivan, Scott Thomas
Research: Mike Barr, Timothy J. Breslin, Cheryl Graham, Barbara Lightner, Loranne Shields
Graphics and Design: Kathy Creech, Sandra Dyrlund, Charlene Epple, Tom Evans
Permissions: Janet Peterson
Indexing: David Pofelski
Prepress and Manufacturing: Anne Dillon, Carma Fazio, Anne Fritzinger, Steven Hueppchen,
    Tina Ramirez
Writer: Dan Blunk

For information about other World Book publications, visit our Web site at http://www.worldbook.com or call 1-800-WORLDBK (967-5325).

For information about sales to schools and libraries, call 1-800-975-3250 (United States); 1-800-837-5365 (Canada).

World Book, Inc.
233 N. Michigan Avenue
Chicago, IL 60601
U.S.A.

Library of Congress Cataloging-in-Publication Data

Silkies and other guinea pigs.
    p. cm. -- (World Book's animals of the world)
  Summary: "An introduction to Silkies and Other Guinea Pigs,
presented in a highly illustrated, question and answer format.
Features include fun facts, glossary, resource list, index, and
scientific classification list"--Provided by publisher.
  Includes bibliographical references.
  ISBN-13: 978-0-7166-1334-3
  ISBN-10: 0-7166-1334-4
  1. Guinea pigs--Miscellanea--Juvenile literature. I. Series.
SF401.G85S55 2007
636.935'92--dc22
                    2006017464

Printed in Malaysia
1 2 3 4 5 6 7 8 09 08 07 06

Picture Acknowledgments: Cover: © Hawkes Photography; © Paul Laing, Alamy Images; © Ken Lucas, Ardea London; © Jorg & Petra Wegner, Animals Animals; © Maximilian Weinzierl, Alamy Images.

© Paul Bricknell, Dorling Kindersley 3, 23, 29, 35; © Peter Cade, Stone/Getty Images 27; © Simon Colmer and Abby Rex, Alamy Images 57; © John Daniels, Ardea London 53; © Pat Haefele 4, 5, 37, 41, 43; © Hawkes Photography 45; © imagebroker/Alamy Images 5, 15; © Juniors Bildarchiv/Alamy Images 19; © Jutta Klee, Photodisc/Getty Images 47; © Richard Kolar, Animals Animals 7; © Jean Michel Labat, Ardea London 25, 49, 51; © Paul Laing, Alamy Images 21; © Ken Lucas, Ardea London 13;

© Darren Matthews, Alamy Images 23; © Carolyn A. McKeone 39; © Carolyn A. McKeone, Photo Researchers 59; © Renee Morris, Alamy Images 33; © Rhoda Peacher 31; © Jorg & Petra Wegner, Animals Animals 61; © Maximilian Weinzierl, Alamy Images 17, 55.

Illustrations: WORLD BOOK illustrations by John Fleck 9.

Silkies
and Other Guinea Pigs

World Book, Inc.
a Scott Fetzer company
Chicago

Contents

What Is a Guinea Pig?

Guinea pigs are small, furry animals with shiny eyes and plump bodies. They are smaller than a cat, but larger than a mouse.

A guinea pig is a mammal—a type of animal that feeds its young with milk made by the mother. Guinea pigs belong to a group of animals called rodents (gnawing mammals). Other rodents include mice, hamsters, and gerbils. A guinea pig is a type of rodent called a cavy *(KAY vee)*.

Guinea pigs can make great pets because they are very cuddly and sweet-tempered. Once they are comfortable in their new home, pet guinea pigs enjoy attention and are relatively easy to care for. But even though guinea pigs are fairly easy to keep, it is important to take the right steps to help your pet stay healthy and happy.

A Silky

What Are Those Long Teeth For?

Like all rodents, guinea pigs have two top and two bottom front teeth, which are called incisors *(ihn SY zuhrz)*. Incisors keep growing throughout a guinea pig's life. These teeth do, however, wear away at the tips, and they wear faster in the back than in front. As a result, incisors have a chisellike edge, well suited to gnawing. By eating coarse foods like grass, the guinea pig keeps its teeth worn down to the height that is best for chewing (see page 54). Behind the incisors, other teeth called premolars and molars are used to crush and grind food.

A guinea pig has a large head, small ears, short legs, and a small, plump body.

Most guinea pigs that live in their natural surroundings have long, coarse, brown or gray fur. Guinea pigs bred by people may have long or short fur of varying texture. The animals may be black, brown, red, white, or a combination of colors.

8

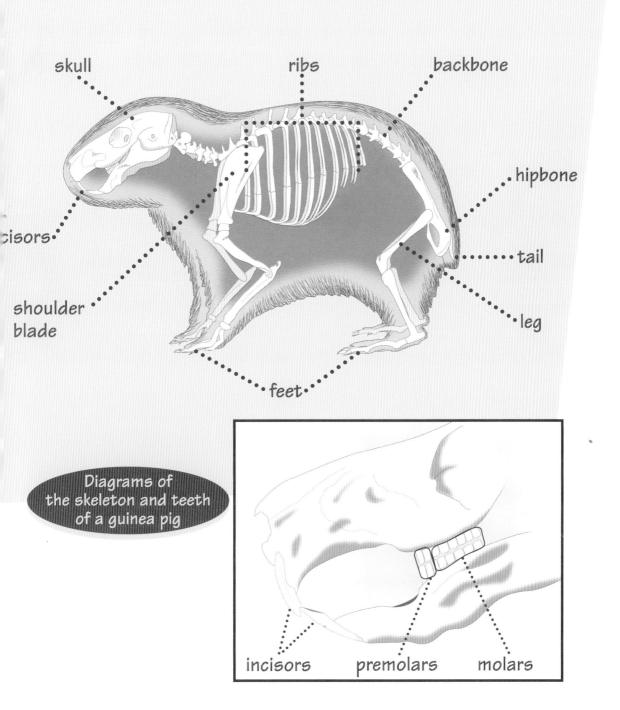

skull

ribs

backbone

hipbone

tail

leg

incisors

shoulder blade

feet

Diagrams of the skeleton and teeth of a guinea pig

incisors

premolars

molars

9

Where Did Guinea Pigs First Live?

The kind of of guinea pig most often kept as a pet is descended from wild guinea pigs that still live in South America today. These wild guinea pigs live in the mountains and the flat grasslands of South America, as well as at the edges of forests and in marshes and rocky areas.

For thousands of years, people in South America used guinea pigs for food. In the 1500's, travelers from other parts of the world explored Peru and took guinea pigs back to their homelands. After this, people began keeping guinea pigs as pets.

Pet guinea pigs live in many countries today, but all guinea pigs can be traced back to the guinea pigs of South America.

A map showing where guinea pigs first lived

North America

Equator

Africa

South America

Atlantic Ocean

Pacific Ocean

Southern Ocean

Antarctica

11

What Are Wild Guinea Pigs Like?

Guinea pigs in the wild usually live in small groups of between 5 and 10 animals. This group of guinea pigs will usually eat, sleep, and rest together. The group shares a territory and acts as a community, warning members within the group of danger. When they become frightened, guinea pigs produce loud, whistlelike screams.

Wild guinea pigs make their homes in the crevices of rocks, in shrubbery, or in burrows (holes dug in the ground) left by other animals. Sometimes wild guinea pigs live in fields of tall grass.

Wild guinea pigs spend much of their time eating, grooming themselves, resting, and playing. Guinea pigs are most active at night.

A wild guinea pig

How Did Breeds of Guinea Pigs Develop?

There are many different breeds of pet guinea pigs. A breed is a group of animals that have the same type of ancestors. All breeds of guinea pigs are related to wild cousins living in South America. When people domesticated (tamed) guinea pigs, they began breeding the guinea pigs for certain desired physical traits, such as hair of a certain color or length.

For example, long-haired guinea pigs are the result of breeders mating guinea pigs that had hair slightly longer than the hair of ordinary guinea pigs. Breeders selected guinea pigs with longer hair and mated them for many generations. Over many years, breeders developed guinea pigs with very long hair.

Silkies, which are also called shelties, are a breed of guinea pig. They were bred to have long hair on their body but short hair on their face. The hair on a Silky's face does not cover its eyes.

Guinea pigs of three
different breeds

How Big Do Guinea Pigs Get? How Long Do They Live?

Young guinea pigs are so small that an adult could easily hold two of them in one hand. But guinea pigs do not stay that small for long. They grow up so quickly that they can reach full size in about a year.

Full-sized guinea pigs can be anywhere from about 10 to 14 inches (25 to 36 centimeters) long. An adult guinea pig will usually weigh between 2 and 3 pounds (0.9 and 1.4 kilograms).

Guinea pigs do not usually live as long as pet cats and dogs often do. Still, if you take very good care of your guinea pig, it can live as long as seven or eight years. Some guinea pigs live even longer.

A guinea pig and a budgie

17

What Kind of Personality Might a Silky Guinea Pig Have?

Like most guinea pigs, Silkies are usually very tame. Silkies and other guinea pigs rarely, if ever, bite people.

Silkies like to play with their owners and with other guinea pigs, but they are also happy resting in their cages. Silkies enjoy being held by their owners.

Some Silkies like having their long fur brushed regularly. In addition to making the Silkies feel good, brushing also makes it easier to keep them clean.

A playful Silky

What Should You Look for When Choosing a Guinea Pig?

Pick a guinea pig that is lively and that has bright, clear eyes. Also, look closely at the guinea pig's coat of hair. If the hair is thin or falling out, the guinea pig may be sick and will not make a good pet.

Make sure your guinea pig's upper teeth just slightly overlap its lower teeth. If the teeth do not overlap, the guinea pig may have trouble eating. You should also avoid choosing any guinea pig with teeth that are crooked or out of place; that animal might eventually have health problems.

Both young and old guinea pigs make good pets. A young guinea pig should be at least four weeks old to become a pet. At this age, a guinea pig is no longer dependent on its mother for food. If you choose a female that is more than four weeks old, however, there is a risk that she may already be pregnant (expecting young). Guinea pigs reproduce at a very early age.

A healthy guinea pig

What Does a
Guinea Pig Eat?

Guinea pigs are herbivores *(HUR buh vawrz)*. This means they only eat grasses and other plants. Your guinea pig's diet should consist mostly of vegetables and food pellets made especially for guinea pigs.

Vegetables that are especially good for guinea pigs are cauliflower, broccoli, curly kale, endive, romaine lettuce, and cabbage. Fruits, such as apples and melons, should be an occasional treat.

Your guinea pig's diet should be rich in vitamin C. Guinea pigs are not able to make this vitamin themselves and must get it from their food. You may add drops of vitamin C to the animal's water supply.

Guinea pigs also must have a steady supply of hay to eat. A rack to hold hay in your pet's cage can be purchased at a pet supply store. The rack keeps the hay off the floor of the cage so it will be clean and fresh for the animal to eat.

Your animal also needs fresh water in its cage. A drip-feed water bottle is best for your guinea pig.

Guinea pigs eat only plant foods

GUINEA PIG

Where Should a Pet Guinea Pig Be Kept?

Pet guinea pigs that are kept indoors usually live and sleep in a cage. Most people keep guinea pigs in wire cages because they are easy to clean.

A guinea pig's cage should be well ventilated and needs to be at least 24 inches (61 centimeters) high, wide, and long. The cage should be kept in an area that is free of drafts. Make sure that the cage does not have a wire floor because that can hurt your guinea pig's feet. Most pet stores sell wire cages with plastic bottoms.

Keep a layer of bedding, such as clean hay, on the floor of the cage. Also, put a small box or tube in the cage where your guinea pig can rest or hide when it wants a quiet place.

Pet guinea pigs should be kept in a cage

25

How Do You Groom a Guinea Pig?

Guinea pigs generally keep themselves clean and neat, but some guinea pigs need help taking care of their nails and hair.

Wild guinea pigs use their nails to dig, and this keeps the nails short. Pet guinea pigs may not dig enough for the nails to become worn down. A guinea pig's nails should be clipped when they get too long. Ask an adult to trim your pet's nails for you.

Guinea pigs with short hair usually do not need help keeping their hair neat. But guinea pigs with long hair do. You should brush or comb a long-haired guinea pig several times a week. You may use an old, discarded comb or brush or purchase one from a pet store. Brush the hair on the guinea pig's back away from its head. Also gently brush its belly.

Long-haired guinea pigs
need regular brushing

Should You Give a Guinea Pig a Bath?

Guinea pigs keep themselves clean and seldom smell bad, so most guinea pigs never need a bath. But some long-haired guinea pigs may occasionally need a bath if their hair gets very dirty. A guinea pig should not be bathed more than once every three months, as frequent baths can dry out its skin.

If your guinea pig does need a bath, place your pet carefully in a large bowl used only for this purpose. Pour lukewarm water over the guinea pig's body using a cup or jug. Use a mild shampoo made for animals. Gently rub the shampoo into the guinea pig's coat. Pour clean water over the guinea pig to rinse it off. Make sure to keep the soap out of your guinea pig's eyes and ears.

When you are done, wrap your guinea pig in a towel and gently pat it dry. This will help to keep your pet warm. Use a hair dryer set on low to dry your guinea pig's hair. If your guinea pig dislikes being blown dry, let its hair dry naturally, but keep your guinea pig warm and safe until it is dry. Becoming chilled can make guinea pigs more prone to infections.

A long-haired guinea pig gets a bath

29

What Kinds of Exercise or Play Are Needed?

Guinea pigs should be taken out of their cage every day for exercise. But it is also good for your guinea pig (and fun for you) to take your pet out of its cage just to hold it. Most guinea pigs enjoy being held and love attention.

You can play with guinea pigs outside, but you should set up a small, enclosed area so they can play safely. Make certain that your guinea pig cannot escape from its outdoor enclosure. And, when your guinea pig is outdoors, guard it from dogs, cats, or other animals that could hurt your pet.

If your guinea pig is outside of its cage in your house, make certain it cannot reach any electrical cords. Chewing these cords can be deadly to guinea pigs.

A guinea pig enjoys
playing outdoors

How Do You Help a Guinea Pig Care for Its Young?

It is a good idea to keep guinea pigs separated by gender to prevent them from breeding. If, however, a guinea pig should come to you already pregnant, here is what to expect and what to do.

A guinea pig that is pregnant should be kept in a separate cage from male guinea pigs one week before her young are due. In addition to her regular food, a pregnant guinea pig should be fed extra green vegetables.

When the young guinea pigs, called puppies, are born, they have plenty of hair and can open their eyes. Domestic guinea pigs can have litters of up to eight puppies. Wild guinea pigs usually have one to four puppies. Young guinea pigs need their mother's milk for the first three weeks they are alive, but they can also eat solid food after a few days.

Once the litter is 1 month old, separate the males and females, because they could have young of their own very soon.

A mother guinea pig
and her puppies

Is It Okay to Play with a Newborn Guinea Pig?

When guinea pigs are born they weigh about 3 ounces (85 grams). A newborn guinea pig is well developed, with thick hair on its body and its eyes open. Within the first day of its life, a guinea pig is able to run and eat solid food.

Although a very young guinea pig can run, it usually stays close to its mother for several days after it is born. Then, the guinea pig will start to explore. At that point, when a young guinea pig has started to move around more, it is okay to play very gently with it.

Four newborn puppies

What Are Some Other Breeds of Guinea Pig?

Currently, there are 13 breeds of guinea pig recognized by the American Cavy Breeders Association (an organization that sanctions guinea pig shows in the United States). Each breed of guinea pig has distinctive hair and markings. Guinea pigs with hair of all one color are described as having a self pattern. Other guinea pigs have fur patterns described as marked, solid, or agouti *(uh GOO tee),* which is made up of bands of dark and light fur.

There are short-haired and long-haired breeds. Some guinea pigs have shiny coats; others have coarse, rough coats. There are even guinea pigs that have swirls, called rosettes, in their hair.

Long-haired guinea pigs require more grooming than short-haired breeds, but many people like how long hair makes their guinea pig look.

An American
Satin Cream

Who Is as Cute as a Teddy Bear?

The Teddy guinea pig gets its name from the texture and appearance of its coat, which is similar to a teddy bear's fur. An adult Teddy has a coat that is thick and the hairs are bent in such a way as to make them stand straight up.

A Teddy's coat is short, ideally about ¾ inch (1.9 centimeters) in length. Because of their short coat, Teddies do not need to be groomed as often as long-haired guinea pigs do.

There are two varieties of Teddy guinea pigs—plush and harsh. Plush Teddies have a coat of soft, fluffy hair. The coat of harsh Teddies is wiry and a bit longer than the coat of plush Teddies. A harsh Teddy's coat may partly cover its face.

A Teddy

Who Has Flowery Fur?

The Abyssinian *(AB uh SIHN ee uhn)* guinea pig, also called the Aby or Abby, is easily recognized by its unique coat of fur. The coat consists of rosettes— a word used to describe anything that is formed like a rose. On the Aby, these rosettes are sections of swirled hair that spread out in all directions from a central point. Ridges of fur surround these rosettes. An Abyssinian's coat is coarse and short to medium in length. The fur may be a single color or a combination of colors, including brown, gold, red, and white.

Abyssinians are a popular breed of guinea pig. Although Abyssinians may be difficult to groom because their fur grows in so many different directions, they do not require frequent grooming— only once a week to remove loose, dead hair.

An Abyssinian

Who Needs Frequent Grooming?

Peruvian guinea pigs are often kept as pets, but they require extra care and attention. These guinea pigs should be groomed daily.

Peruvian guinea pigs have long, thick hair. A Peruvian's hair usually parts straight down its back. The hair on its head grows forward, covering its large, droopy ears and large eyes. Pet owners often trim the hair around a Peruvian's eyes. Peruvians that are shown in competitions, however, must have all their long hair.

Peruvians are often bathed before a show. When a show Peruvian's hair reaches about 3 inches (7.6 centimeters) long, its owner will often "wrap" the guinea pig's coat. In wrapping, a section of the hair is placed in a piece of cloth or paper towel, then that wrap is bundled using a rubber band. This treatment keeps the hair out of the guinea pig's way and keeps the hair neat and clean. Only when the owner is ready to show a Peruvian are the wraps taken off to display the animal's long, beautiful coat.

A Peruvian

Who Has a Curly Coat?

The first thing you will notice about a Texel guinea pig is its curly coat. Long, thick, soft curls cover the entire body of an adult Texel, even its belly. In fact, Texels without belly curls are not allowed to compete in guinea pig shows in the United States.

Texels have a short, compact body. The head of a Texel is wide and rounded. These guinea pigs are bred in a variety of colors.

Because the Texel's long, curly coat can become easily tangled, it must be groomed often and carefully. Pet owners may have their Texel's coat clipped short so that it is easier to care for. Owners who plan to enter their Texel in a guinea pig show, however, cannot clip their animal's coat and must take special care to keep it in good condition.

A Texel

Are Guinea Pigs Really Pigs?

Some people shorten the name for their pet guinea pigs to just "pigs." Guinea pigs, however, are not related to pigs at all. Guinea pigs are rodents.

No one is sure why this animal is called a guinea pig. Some people think the name came from traders who brought the animals to Europe on ships returning from the African country of Guinea.

Other people think the name comes from a British coin called a guinea, which may have been the amount of money that the guinea pigs were sold for when they were first taken to England from South America.

It is possible that guinea pigs got the last part of their name because they are short and plump and squeal and grunt like pigs.

Guinea pigs look a bit like little pigs

How Should You Pick Up a Guinea Pig?

To pick up a guinea pig, firmly place the palm of your hand on its back. This will steady your pet and keep it from trying to get away. Then slide your other hand under its belly. Make sure to hold the guinea pig firmly in both hands. Lift the guinea pig and bring it close to your body. Do not hold it so tightly that you are squeezing it, but place the guinea pig against your chest so that you do not drop it and it cannot jump out of your hands. Make sure you handle the guinea pig carefully.

Shift your hand from under the belly to the rump. This will help you to provide support to your pet's body and keep it from falling. If you hold it this way, your guinea pig will feel safe when you are handling it.

48

Hold your guinea pig
close to your body

What Kinds of Fun Can You Have with Your Guinea Pig?

Guinea pigs enjoy being out of their cages. You should play with your guinea pig outside of its cage every day.

Enclose a small area on the floor inside your house to make a safe place for your guinea pig to play. You could put a few rocks, boxes, or small, safe toys in the enclosure. You could also put some plastic tubes in the enclosure so your guinea pig has something to run through.

A guinea pig can move very fast, so be sure to watch your pet closely.

Play with your
guinea pig every day

What Kinds of Toys Should Guinea Pigs Play With?

Guinea pigs can play with simple things found in most homes. Many guinea pigs like playing with cardboard tubes, paper bags, and paper cups. Some guinea pigs like straw baskets and cardboard boxes.

Guinea pigs like to run through "tunnels" when they play, so put a collection of plastic or clay pipe sections in their cage. If you have more than one guinea pig, they will enjoy chasing each other through these pipes.

Guinea pigs playing
in flower pots

Can a Guinea Pig's Teeth Get Too Long?

Indeed, they can. A guinea pig's teeth continue to grow for its entire life. You can help your guinea pig keep its teeth healthy and at the right length by giving it things to gnaw on.

If a guinea pig's teeth grow too long, it will not be able to eat and can get sick. To help a guinea pig keep its teeth the right length, give it the type of food that will help it to wear its teeth down. Such foods as hay and other grasses are good for wearing down teeth. When a guinea pig gnaws on these rough foods, it will usually grind its teeth down to the right size for chewing.

If your guinea pig is unable to eat or is losing weight, these could be signs that something is wrong with its teeth. Ask your vet to check. A veterinarian should trim teeth that are seriously overgrown.

A guinea pig gnawing
on a branch

55

What Are Some Common Signs of Illness in Guinea Pigs?

Animals cannot tell people that they are sick or hurt. Still, there are some clues to look for if your guinea pig is not feeling well.

- If your guinea pig is moving slowly, it may not be well. Also, if it does not seem interested in food or water, watch it carefully because it may be ill.

- If your guinea pig develops diarrhea, it could mean your pet has an infection and you should call your veterinarian.

- Check your guinea pig's eyes. If they are cloudy or tearing, your pet could be sick.

- Examine your guinea pig's hair regularly to make sure it is thick and healthy looking. If its coat gets thin and dull or develops bare spots, call your veterinarian.

An inquisitive,
healthy guinea pig

What Routine Veterinary Care Is Needed?

Guinea pigs usually do not require much routine care from a veterinarian, but you should take your guinea pig to the veterinarian's office if it becomes sick or hurt.

You may want to take the guinea pig to the vet soon after you get it so the veterinarian can make sure it is healthy. You can also ask the veterinarian for advice on how to care for your guinea pig.

Contact your veterinarian if your guinea pig starts to act differently from normal—for example, if your pet loses weight, or if it is moving slowly or sitting still for longer periods of time than usual.

A vet checks a
pet guinea pig

59

What Are Your Responsibilities as an Owner?

As the owner of a guinea pig, you are responsible for its health. Your pet depends on you for everything. You must keep its cage clean and make sure your animal gets proper food and exercise.

Guinea pigs are social animals, so you should give your pet attention every day. Also, consider getting more than one guinea pig. It is a good idea, however, to make sure they are both of the same sex.

One of the most important things you can do is to make sure your guinea pig is fed a balanced diet. You should make nutritious food and clean water available to your guinea pig at all times.

Have fun! Your pet guinea pig depends on you, so take good care of it and you will have fun with it for many years to come.

A happy, healthy Silky

Guinea Pig Fun Facts

→ Often, guinea pigs will ignore the toys purchased for them at a pet store. Some items guinea pigs usually do like to play with include paper bags, empty shoe boxes, and crumpled pieces of paper.

→ The guinea pig is related to the largest rodent, the capybara. A capybara may weigh over 100 pounds (45 kilograms).

→ Young guinea pigs are born after developing inside their mother's body for only about 70 days. A human baby needs to develop inside of its mother for somewhere around 266 days.

→ Female guinea pigs are called sows. Males are called boars. A group of guinea pigs is called a herd.

→ To be eligible to be entered in a guinea pig show, an Abyssinian (see page 40) must have at least 8 rosettes in its fur.

62

Glossary

agouti A coat made up of bands of light and dark fur.

breed To produce animals by carefully selecting and mating them for certain traits. Also, a group of animals having the same type of ancestors.

burrow A hole dug in the ground by an animal for refuge or shelter. Also, to dig a hole in the ground.

cavy The name for several related South American rodents. Guinea pigs are the best-known cavies.

domesticate To tame an animal so that it can live with or under the care of humans.

generation In animals, offspring that are at a common stage of descent from the same ancestors. For example, the young born to one set of parents at one time form one generation of guinea pigs.

groom To rub down or brush an animal.

herbivore An animal that feeds on grasses or other plants.

incisor A tooth having a sharp edge for cutting; one of the front teeth in mammals between the canine teeth.

litter The young animals produced by an animal at one birthing.

mammal A type of animal that feeds its young with milk made by the mother.

puppy A young guinea pig.

rodent A type of mammal having two continually growing incisor teeth used for gnawing.

rosette Flowerlike swirls in an animal's hair.

trait A feature or characteristic particular to an animal or breed of animals.

Index

(**Boldface** indicates a photo, map, or illustration.)

For more information about Silkies and Other Guinea Pigs, try these resources:

The Guinea Pig Handbook, by Sharon L. Vanderlip, Barron's Educational Series, 2003

Guinea Pigs, by Mark Evans, Dorling Kindersley Publishing, 2001

101 Facts About Guinea Pigs, by Julia Barnes, Gareth Stevens, 2001

The Proper Care of Guinea Pigs, by Peter Gurney, TFH Publications, 1999

http://www.acbaonline.com/
http://cavyrescue.com/
http://guinealynx.info/

Guinea Pig Classification

Scientists classify animals by placing them into groups. The animal kingdom is a group that contains all the world's animals. Phylum, class, order, and family are smaller groups. Each phylum contains many classes. A class contains orders, an order contains families, and a family contains genuses. One or more species belong to each genus. Each species has its own scientific name. Here is how the animals in this book fit into this system.

Animals with backbones and their relatives (Phylum Chordata)
Mammals (Class Mammalia)
Rodents (Order Rodentia)

Guinea pigs and their relatives (Family Caviidae)

Domestic guinea pig . . . . *Cavia porcellus*